15 Plays About Famous Americans

for Emergent Readers

by Carol Pugliano-Martin

SCHOLASTIC
PROFESSIONAL BOOKS

New York • Toronto • London • Auckland • Sydney
Mexico City • New Delhi • Hong Kong • Buenos Aires

To Hayden, who was with me this time.

And in memory of my dear father, Frank Pugliano,
who was also a great American.

Cover and interior illustrations by George Ulrich

Cover design by Josué Castilleja

Interior design by Sydney Wright

Edited by Kathleen Hollenbeck

ISBN: 0-439-32333-9

Copyright © 2002 by Carol Pugliano-Martin.

Printed in the U.S.A. All rights reserved.

1 2 3 4 5 6 7 8 9 10   40   09 08 07 06 05 04 03 02

Contents

Introduction

What I've enjoyed most about writing this book has been learning more about the fascinating people who have helped shape our country. Their legacies continue to teach and inspire us, from one generation to the next. Learning about these Americans not only helps children learn about the history of our country but also teaches them important lessons that they can apply to their own lives. They can learn from Orville and Wilbur Wright to take creative chances. Susan B. Anthony, Rosa Parks, and Martin Luther King, Jr., teach children to stand up for their beliefs. From Squanto, children can learn to help those who are different from themselves. And who knows how many children will be inspired by Sally Ride to fulfill their dream of becoming an astronaut?

15 Plays About Famous Americans for Emergent Readers provides an interactive and engaging way to introduce children to these important figures in American history while building essential oral language skills. The plays are intended for read-aloud activities rather than student productions, but they work well for either purpose. Designed for emergent readers, the read-aloud plays feature:

- reproducible play scripts with delightful illustrations
- large, easy-to-read text and short sentences
- simple language that includes rhyme, repetition, and predictability
- multiple parts to allow for maximum student participation
- group parts to help beginning readers gain confidence

For each play, you'll find background information and a related activity to extend learning. The activities span a wide variety of curriculum areas including science, writing, and math.

Helpful Hints

- ★ In advance, photocopy the play and distribute a copy to each student.
- ★ Adjust the number of speakers to match your class's needs.
- ★ To give everyone a chance to participate, have students read through the plays several times, changing the cast each time. You may also have students team up to read the same part together.
- ★ Feel free to have girls read male parts and vice versa.
- ★ After assigning parts, hand out crayons or markers so children can highlight their lines.
- ★ Read the play aloud to your class before they read it on their own. This will help familiarize children with the play's content and action. Review any new vocabulary.
- ★ Tape-record students reading aloud and then play back the tape as children follow along in the text.
- ★ Ask children to identify rhyming language or refrains.
- ★ Invite children to act out the plays using simple props.
- ★ Encourage children to take home their play scripts to read with family members.
- ★ Put on simple productions of the plays for Visitors' Day.

As I write this, I am expecting my second son. It's fun to envision him being old enough to learn about these famous Americans. By the time he is an adult, there will be other famous Americans to learn about, and perhaps my son will be one of them. Maybe some future famous Americans are sitting in your classroom right now!

—*Carol Pugliano-Martin*

Background and Activities

Christopher Columbus

1451–1506

Born in Genoa, Italy, Christopher Columbus is credited with being the first European to reach the New World. In 1492 Columbus traveled from Spain to America. At that time, people sailed east from Europe to get to the Orient. Columbus felt that he could reach the Orient faster by sailing west instead. Queen Isabella and King Ferdinand of Spain funded his voyage, supplying him with about 90 sailors and three ships: the *Niña*, the *Pinta*, and the *Santa Maria*. Two months into the journey, Columbus and his crew stepped ashore onto an island. Columbus believed they had reached an island off the coast of Asia, but it was really southeast of present-day Florida. He later named the island San Salvador. There the crew encountered a Native American group, the Arawaks. Columbus traded goods with the Arawaks, giving them glass beads, brass rings, and bells in exchange for parrots, cotton, and hunting spears. Since Columbus thought he had reached the Indies, he named the Arawaks "Indians." We remember Columbus's determination and courage, but his arrival in North America held few positive consequences for the Arawaks.

Terrific Treasure Maps (Social Studies)

Remind your students that Christopher Columbus became an expert at reading maps. Provide children with an opportunity to practice reading and following maps. Divide the class into groups of three to four students. Invite each group to hide a "treasure" (such as a chalk eraser or a toy) in the classroom and design a map that will help another group find it. You may want to model the activity beforehand, pointing out areas in the classroom that students might include on their maps. Make sure each group labels their map with key areas in the room and draws a clear route to the object, with or without a map key. Then have the groups take turns imagining they are explorers as they read the maps to find the hidden objects.

Desire Minter

c. 1605–1650

Desire Minter was one of about 30 children aboard the *Mayflower*. She was 15 years old when the *Mayflower* left Plymouth, England, in September 1620. During the voyage, there was not much for children to do. They had to leave most of their toys behind. The children amused themselves by telling stories, singing songs, and playing "I Spy." They also had responsibilities aboard the ship, such as cooking, cleaning, and tending to sick passengers. They ate mostly salted beef, as well as fish, peas, oatmeal, cheese, butter, a hard bread called ship's biscuit, and dried fruit such as raisins and prunes. Due to storms, seasickness, and disease, the trip was difficult. Desire and the rest of the *Mayflower* passengers arrived in Provincetown, Massachusetts, on November 21, 1620. They then moved on and settled in what is now Plymouth.

Pilgrim "I-Spy" (Language Arts)

Play one of the games that Desire Minter and her friends enjoyed on board the *Mayflower*. To play, ask one volunteer to look around the classroom and secretly choose an object. The player must then say, "I spy something that is _____," using one word to describe the shape, color, purpose, or location of the item. Based on the clue (and other clues, as needed), classmates guess the identity of the object. If your students are familiar with the *Mayflower*, you may want to have them pretend they are Pilgrims who are actually playing the game aboard the ship. Show students illustrations of the *Mayflower* to give them ideas of things they might have found on board, such as a sail, a ship's wheel, clothing, or water.

Interviews of Interest (Prereading)

"On the *Mayflower*" is written in interview format. Interviews offer a great way for students to get to know one another. Create a simple interview sheet for children. Leave space at the top of the page for children to write or dictate an interview question and draw a picture to go with it. Below the space, make two columns labeled "Yes" and "No." Give children each a copy of the interview sheet and explain that they should write or dictate a question to ask classmates that requires a yes or no answer, such as "Do you like ice cream?" "Do you have a pet?" or "Do you ride the bus to school?" (You may want to brainstorm a list of questions with students beforehand.) Then have children draw a picture that represents the question. The drawings might be an ice cream cone, a dog, and so on. Show children how to make tally marks. Then invite them to take turns interviewing classmates and marking their responses with tally marks in the appropriate columns.

Squanto

c. 1585–1622

Squanto was a Pawtuxet Indian who lived in what is now Massachusetts. In 1615 Squanto was kidnapped by the English. He lived in England for several years. When he returned home, he found that his whole village had been wiped out by disease, so he joined the Wampanoag. Squanto met the Pilgrims when they settled near his former home. Because Squanto could speak English, he was able to help the Pilgrims in many ways. He taught them effective ways to plant corn, catch eels, hunt, and find food in the forest. He also helped the Pilgrims negotiate a peace treaty with the Wampanoag, which lasted more than 60 years.

Handy Helpers (Social Studies/Citizenship)

Have children sit in a circle for this activity. First, explain that Squanto was able to help the Pilgrims because he had skills they needed to learn. Lead a discussion about ways your students can be helpers, too. Ask students to think of something they do well in school. It doesn't have to be an academic subject; it can be drawing, block-building, climbing on the jungle gym, tying shoes, playing a sport, and so on. Go around the circle and have each child name his or her skill. As children are sharing, write their names and skills on the chalkboard or on chart paper. Then invite children to look at the list and find at least one child who can help them with a skill they would like to improve. Help match students so that each child has a chance to be a helper. Sharing their special knowledge and talent will help children feel empowered while fostering an atmosphere of cooperation in your classroom.

George Washington

1732–1799

George Washington is known as "The Father of Our Country." He commanded the Continental Army in America's fight against Great Britain for independence. In 1787 Washington served as president of the Constitutional Convention in Philadelphia. In 1789, despite his desire to retire to his home in Virginia, he was elected the first president of the United States. Although many Americans wanted George Washington to be king, Washington insisted on maintaining a government with shared power and in which United States citizens had a voice. After serving two terms as president, George Washington retired to his plantation in Virginia, where he died in 1799.

Our Important Firsts (Prewriting/Writing)

George Washington accomplished a very important "first"—being the first president of the United States. What important firsts have your students accomplished? Examples may include riding a two-wheeler, losing a tooth, or reading a book by themselves. Invite children to draw pictures of their important firsts and to write or dictate a sentence or two describing the event. Encourage students to share their work with the class, and then make a collaborative book with the pages.

Betsy Ross

1752–1836

Betsy Ross was a seamstress whom some historians credit with making the first official United States flag. It is known that she worked as a flag maker for the Pennsylvania Navy. According to William J. Canby, a grandson of Betsy Ross, she was asked by General George Washington to sew a United States flag in 1776. Canby reported that his 84-year-old grandmother told him that Washington visited her upholstery shop in May of that year, asking her to make a flag based on a design that he showed her. At the time, General Washington was head of the Continental Army. Two influential men accompanied him, a wealthy landowner named Robert Morris and Colonel George Ross, the uncle of Betsy Ross's late husband. Betsy Ross accepted the assignment and completed the flag within a month's time. On June 14, 1777, the Continental Congress adopted the flag design that Ross is said to have sewn.

Make Your Own Flags (Art)

Explain that the symbols on the United States flag stand for the 13 original colonies and the 50 states. Show students pictures of the flag at different points in time to demonstrate how it has changed over time to reflect the growth of our country. Invite children to design a flag to represent themselves. What symbols would students use to describe themselves? Encourage them to include symbols that represent their skills, hobbies, characteristics, and other important aspects of their personalities. Display the finished flags without students' names on them; then challenge students to guess whose flag is whose.

Johnny Appleseed

1774–1845

The folk hero Johnny Appleseed was a real man who spent his life planting apple seeds and tending orchards across Ohio and Indiana. Born John Chapman in Leominster, Massachusetts, he earned his nickname by planting apple seeds in the wilderness from 1797 until his death in 1845. His plantings became full apple orchards, which eventually supplied food for the settlers. As John traveled west, he became well known for his kindness to people and animals as well as his eccentric lifestyle, which included walking barefoot and living outdoors, in barns, and in livestock pens. Legend has it that John wore a cooking pot on his head to free his hands so he could hold a book.

Sums of Seeds (Math)

Give each child six to ten apple seeds. Have children write or dictate math facts based on the number of seeds. For example, they could write one or more of the following math facts for seven seeds: $1 + 6 = 7$; $2 + 5 = 7$; $3 + 4 = 7$; $4 + 3 = 7$; $5 + 2 = 7$; $6 + 1 = 7$

Students can also rearrange their seeds to demonstrate subtraction problems. Once children have finished writing or dictating their math facts, have them glue the seeds onto paper.

Abraham Lincoln

1809–1865

Abraham Lincoln was the sixteenth president of the United States. Possessing superior intelligence, composure, and common sense, he is remembered as one of our country's greatest leaders. His eloquent speeches and honest demeanor, even in his youth, attracted the attention and admiration of many. Of the four men who ran for president in 1860, Lincoln was the only one who stood firmly against the spread of slavery. As president, he led the country through one of the most difficult periods of United States history: the Civil War. Determined to abolish slavery and unite the nation, Lincoln succeeded in doing both. He sent northern forces to war against southern states rather than allow the southern states to secede and form their own nation. He also passed the Emancipation Proclamation, freeing slaves and putting an end to bondage. Just five days after the Civil War ended, Lincoln was shot and killed by John Wilkes Booth. He was the first United States president to be assassinated.

Acts of Kindness (Social Studies/Citizenship)

Since his youth, Abraham Lincoln was known to be honest and kind. To encourage these characteristics in your classroom, create an "Acts of Kindness" chart to display all year long. Invite children to write on a slip of paper every time they witness an act of kindness among their classmates. At the end of each day or week, review the papers and write all or some of these acts on the chart. Some examples might be helping someone tie his or her shoes, sharing a snack, or complimenting someone on an accomplishment. In May or June, hold a kindness ceremony and read aloud all the wonderful deeds your students have performed throughout the year.

Harriet Tubman

c. 1820–1913

Harriet Tubman helped more than 300 slaves escape to freedom. Born into slavery in Bucktown, Maryland, she was given the name Araminta Ross. As a child, she took her mother's name, which was Harriet. Tubman escaped from slavery in 1849 by following the Underground Railroad north. She left her husband and family behind and made the journey alone to Pennsylvania. Tubman traveled at night and rested during the day. When nights were clear, she followed the North Star to find her way. When this wasn't possible, she determined which direction was north by feeling tree trunks for moss (moss grows on the north side of trees).

Once Tubman reached the North, she decided to become a "conductor" of the Underground Railroad and lead others to freedom. Tubman returned to the South many times, leading family, friends, and many other slaves to freedom. During the Civil War, she tended wounded soldiers and gathered important information for the Union Army. She died in 1913 in Auburn, New York, when she was more than 90 years old.

Constellation Creations (Science)

Explain to children that the Underground Railroad was neither a railroad nor was it underground. It was a term given to the escape route of slaves from the South to the North. People who helped hide slaves along the way were called stationmasters and their houses were called stations. Those who led the way, like Harriet Tubman, were conductors. Because conductors and passengers traveled mainly at night, they relied on stars to show them which way was north. Show children a map of the constellations. Point out the North Star (Polaris), which was the main star the slaves followed. Explain how to find the North Star by drawing an imaginary line northward from the two stars at the front of the cup of the Big Dipper to the bright star on the end, which is the North Star. Due to its position in the sky, the North Star appears to stand still while the other stars seem to revolve around the earth's axis, making it a reliable tool for navigation. Also point out other constellations, and ask students why they think each constellation might have been assigned its name. Then encourage students to draw their own constellations. Using construction paper, sequins, and glue, invite students to arrange their "stars" (sequins) into shapes (animals, people, or objects). Children can then name their constellations and share them with the class.

Susan B. Anthony

1820–1906

Born in 1820 in Adams, Massachusetts, Susan B. Anthony always felt a strong sense of justice and morality, even when she was a little girl. As a child, Anthony observed her parents' involvement in antislavery movements. As an adult, she continued their work. She also became involved in the temperance movement, supporting tougher liquor laws. Anthony's attention turned to women's rights in 1852 when she attended her first feminist convention in Syracuse. A year later her commitment to the cause of women's rights intensified when she was not allowed to speak at a temperance rally because she was a woman and when a petition she had helped generate was rejected because it contained the signatures of mostly women and children. Anthony realized that women needed the right to vote so politicians would listen to them. With the inspiration of Elizabeth Cady Stanton, a leader in the women's rights movement, Anthony dedicated her life to women's rights, campaigning for the cause until her death in 1906. In 1920 American women were given the right to vote with the adoption of the Nineteenth Amendment, which is also known as the Susan B. Anthony Amendment.

Cast Your Vote! (Social Studies)

Provide children with the experience of voting in your classroom. Whenever there is a choice to be made during the day, hold a classroom vote. Classroom votes will allow your students to experience democracy in action firsthand. After you have held several class votes, lead a discussion about the experience. Ask children how they made their decisions and how they felt about voting. Did they ever cast a vote in favor of something that was voted down? How did they feel? What other decisions would they like to influence through voting? How would they feel if they were not allowed to vote? How do they think Susan B. Anthony felt?

George Washington Carver

c. 1864–1943

Born a slave in Missouri, George Washington Carver is best known for his scientific work with peanuts. As head of the Tuskegee Institute's agricultural department, Carver researched soil conservation and crop growth improvement. When southern farmers found that boll weevils were destroying their cotton plants and that the soil was becoming unhealthy due to overuse, Carver suggested planting peanuts and sweet potatoes, plants that would resist pests and rejuvenate the soil. Through his research, he also discovered more than 300 products that could be created from peanuts, including peanut milk, flour, shampoo, ice cream, and ink. In addition, he discovered 118 products that could be made from sweet potatoes, such as sweet potato glue, flour, and syrup. Thanks to Carver's work, the farms of many African-Americans of the South were saved. George Washington Carver was a professor at the Tuskegee Institute for 47 years.

Foods With Many Uses (Science)

What other foods besides peanuts have multiple uses? Allow students to choose a food and brainstorm various ways the food is and might be used. Examples of such foods include eggs, rice, bread, and oatmeal. Encourage students to be creative in thinking about how different foods might be used. Have children work in groups and then present their ideas to the class.

The Wright Brothers

Orville *Wilbur*
1871–1948 *1867–1912*

As young boys, Orville and Wilbur Wright loved to build things, especially kites. They often sold kites to their friends. When the brothers grew up, they built and sold their own bicycles. Eventually, they became interested in flight and began building models of gliders. They dreamed of building a glider that could hold a person. Neighbors thought it was funny that grown men would spend their time on what they thought was a silly invention, but the Wright brothers succeeded. Later they set to work on inventing a motorized glider. On December 17, 1903, in Kitty Hawk, North Carolina, their hard work paid off. They made the first motor-powered flight. Its effects were long-reaching: Today's airplanes still run on principles used by the very first flying machine.

Try and Try Again! (Science)

The Wright Brothers, like most scientists, tested their work over and over again before they met with success. Give your students firsthand experience at the magic of flight through trial and error. Divide the class into pairs. Give each pair a sheet of 8½- by 11-inch paper. Invite pairs to experiment with making their own paper airplane, using trial and error to achieve success. Encourage them to test their planes and then tailor them as needed to ensure a straight, sturdy flight. Students may need to refold their planes, attach paper clips as weights, or make tiny slits in the plane's nose or wings to adjust its flight pattern. Afterward, have children talk about the results and what might have contributed to a successful or unsuccessful flight.

Helen Keller

1880–1968

Helen Keller was a healthy child at birth. When she was 19 months old, she contracted a disease that caused her to become deaf, blind, and unable to speak. As a young child, she used charadelike movements to communicate. When Keller was nearly seven years old, her parents hired a private teacher, Anne Sullivan, to teach her better ways to communicate. Sullivan taught Keller words by using a finger alphabet and spelling them into her pupil's hand. After much practice, Keller finally understood her first word: *water*. She later said that learning that word gave her light, hope, and joy. She learned to read Braille and eventually to speak, although her voice was not generally intelligible. With Sullivan at her side translating lectures, Helen Keller attended and graduated with honors from Radcliffe College. She then went on to write many books, give lectures, and appear before legislatures to help improve conditions for the blind and deaf. In 1964 Keller was awarded the Presidential Medal of Freedom.

Tune In to the Senses (Science)

Before Helen Keller learned to use sign language and speak, she had to find other ways to communicate. She relied heavily on movement and her senses of touch and smell. The following activities encourage children to use different senses and different methods of communication.

◆ Ask students to sit in a circle and close their eyes. Tell them that they will pass different objects around the circle without speaking. Start by passing a soft object, such as a stuffed

animal, around the circle. Then pass something rough, such as a rock or a piece of sandpaper. If necessary, remind students not to peek. After passing around a few more objects with different textures, have children open their eyes and discuss the objects that they felt. What were they? How did they know? How did the objects feel? How did they know it was their turn to hold each item?

◆ Play a game of charades with your class. Have students use their hands and bodies to convey requests they might have if they were young children at home. Such requests might include wanting to drink a glass of milk, go to bed, or take a bath. You might have students work with partners for this activity.

Martin Luther King, Jr.

1929–1968

Martin Luther King, Jr., was born in Atlanta, Georgia, in 1929. Even as a young boy, he noticed that African-Americans were treated differently from white people. King wanted to change this using peaceful means. He became a minister, and he preached that African-Americans should not use violence in the struggle to win civil rights. In Montgomery, Alabama, King became involved in the Montgomery Bus Boycott. When the boycott was over, King was famous for his nonviolent efforts in leading the Civil Rights movement. In 1963 he organized a peaceful march on Washington to demand equal rights for African-Americans. More than 200,000 people came. It was there that King gave his famous "I Have a Dream" speech. King's efforts helped pass laws against segregation, and in 1964 he was awarded the Nobel Peace Prize. King was assassinated on April 4, 1968. Martin Luther King, Jr., is remembered each year on or around his birthday (January 15), which is a national holiday.

Living the Dream (Social Studies)

Martin Luther King, Jr., dreamed of racial equality to make this country a better place. Encourage your students to write a letter to the president, stating their dreams for a better country. You may post children's letters and then mail them to the White House, using the following address:

> The President of the United States
> The White House
> 1600 Pennsylvania Avenue NW
> Washington, DC 20500

Rosa Parks

Born in 1913

Known as "The Mother of the Civil Rights Movement," Rosa Parks became famous after a bus ride she took in Montgomery, Alabama, on December 1, 1955. In those times, segregation was the law. African-Americans were forced to sit at the back of bus. On that day, Parks was sitting in the middle of the bus, where African-Americans were allowed to sit as long as no white passengers needed their seats. The bus was full when some white people boarded the vehicle. The bus driver told Parks and three other African-Americans to move to the back. The others

12

did so, but Parks refused. She was arrested and put in jail. This event made so many African-Americans angry that they refused to ride the Montgomery buses. Their nonviolent protest was led by Dr. Martin Luther King, Jr., and lasted more than a year. Finally, on November 13, 1956, the United States Supreme Court ruled that segregation on public buses was against the law. A month later, desegregated buses rolled down the streets of Montgomery for the first time. In 1999 Parks was awarded the Congressional Gold Medal of Honor, the highest honor a United States civilian can receive.

Acting Out Compassion (Drama)

Ask your class if they, like Rosa Parks, have ever stood up for something in which they believed. If there are students in the class who have done this, encourage them to act out the event, with volunteers playing the other parts. You may want to help students write the sequence of events on a chalkboard or on chart paper so the actors can refer to it during their scene. After the performance, discuss what happened in the scene. Ask the class whether or not they think the situation was handled in the best way. Invite them to come up with alternative endings. (You might have each group perform their scene and have them freeze at the height of the conflict. Ask the students watching the scene to suggest a resolution to the problem, and then have the performers act it out.) As a class, create a list of other situations in which someone stood up for something he or she believed in, and act those out.

Sally Ride

Born in 1951

Sally Ride was the first American woman to travel into space. She was born on May 26, 1951, near Los Angeles, California, and loved science from the start. While finishing her Ph.D. at Stanford University in California, she answered an ad for astronauts that NASA had put in the campus newspaper. Ride was chosen from about 8,000 applicants. After years of hard training, she was ready for her first mission. She was one of five astronauts aboard the *Challenger* space shuttle STS-7. With the rest of the crew, she took off on June 18, 1983, and landed on June 24. Sally Ride loved the view from space and was quoted as saying "The sparkling oceans and bright orange deserts are glorious against the blackness of space." She also noted that countries have no physical borders from space, making the world look united over land and sea. In 1984 Ride flew another mission, but following the *Challenger* explosion in 1986, in which all passengers died including teacher Christa McAuliffe, she resigned from the astronaut program. Ride took other jobs with NASA and eventually became a professor of physics at the University of California and director of the California Space Institute.

A View From Space (Language Arts)

Tell children that Sally Ride described seeing orange deserts and sparkling seas from the space shuttle. What else might she have seen from that distance? Invite students to pretend they are astronauts traveling through space. What do they see on their way? What do they see when they reach their destination? Invite students to write descriptive words that tell what they see. Guide them to use the words in a poem, a haiku, or a brief story. Have students use pastel chalk on black construction paper to illustrate their writing. As an alternative, provide blank index cards and invite students to make postcards from space, drawing and writing about what they have seen.

Columbus Sails West

Characters

Narrator 1   King (King Ferdinand)

Narrator 2   Queen (Queen Isabella)

Narrator 3   Sailor 1

Columbus (Christopher Columbus)   Sailor 2

Narrator 1: Long ago, people sailed east from Europe to get to India and China.

Narrator 2: Columbus thought he knew a better way. He wanted to sail west.

Narrator 3: Columbus needed money for his trip.

Narrator 1: He asked the king and queen of Spain for help.

Columbus: Dear King and Queen,
I think I know best.
We should not sail east.
We should sail west.

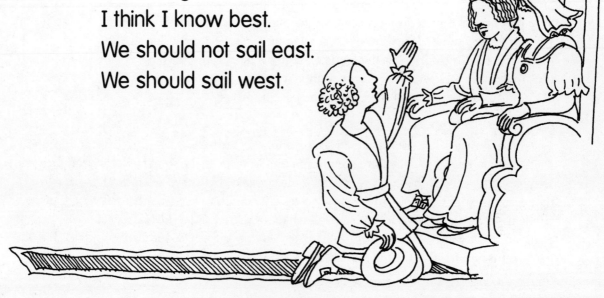

King: No, Columbus.
We do not agree with you.

Queen: We will not pay
for what you want to do.

Narrator 2: Columbus asked the king and queen two more times.

Narrator 3: Finally they agreed to help him.

King: Okay, Columbus.
We will pay for your trip.

Queen: Go ahead. You may start loading your ship.

Narrator 1: So Columbus sailed west.
He took three ships and 90 sailors with him.

Narrator 2: The ships were named
the <u>Niña</u>, the <u>Pinta</u>, and the <u>Santa Maria</u>.

Narrator 3: Some sailors were afraid.
They had never sailed west before.

Sailor 1: I want to go home!

Sailor 2: This is no place for me.

Columbus: Stay strong! We will soon reach dry land.
You will see!

Narrator 1: Columbus and his crew sailed for two months.
Finally, they spotted land.

Narrator 2: Columbus thought they had reached the East Indies,
but they had not.

Narrator 3: They were in the land we now call America!

Narrator 1: The sailors met the Native Americans who lived there.

Narrator 2: They traded goods with them.

Narrator 3: Each year on Columbus Day,
we remember Columbus's brave voyage.

The End

On the *Mayflower*

Characters

Teacher	Student 2
Student 1	Student 3
Desire Minter	

Teacher: If Desire Minter were here
for just one day,
what would you ask her?
What would you say?

Student 1: What did you play
during the day
on the <u>Mayflower</u>,
on the <u>Mayflower</u>?

Desire: There were not many toys
for us girls and boys
on the <u>Mayflower</u>,
on the <u>Mayflower</u>.

We talked and sang songs.
The days seemed so long
on the <u>Mayflower</u>,
on the <u>Mayflower</u>.

Student 2: What did you eat?
Were there any treats
on the <u>Mayflower</u>,
on the <u>Mayflower</u>?

Desire: Salted beef and dry bread
is what we were fed
on the <u>Mayflower</u>,
on the <u>Mayflower</u>.

Student 3: What did you wear
when you were there
on the <u>Mayflower</u>,
on the <u>Mayflower</u>?

Desire: We wore clothes that were warm
in case of a storm
on the <u>Mayflower</u>,
on the <u>Mayflower</u>.

We will always remember
our long, hard trip
on the <u>Mayflower</u>,
on the <u>Mayflower</u>.

The End

Squanto Helps the Pilgrims

Characters

Narrator 1	Pilgrim 3
Narrator 2	Squanto
Pilgrim 1	Chief (Chief Massasoit)
Pilgrim 2	Governor (Governor John Carver)

Narrator 1: Our story opens in Plymouth, Massachusetts.
It is the spring of 1621.

Narrator 2: A Native American stands at the edge of a forest.
He watches some Pilgrims.

Pilgrim 1: The winter was long and hard.
Many of our people died from cold and lack of food.

Pilgrim 2: More will die soon
if we don't learn how to live on this land.

Pilgrim 3: We have searched for food but have found none.
We can't even catch fish! What will we do?

Squanto: I come in peace. My name is Squanto.

Pilgrim 1: You speak English!

Squanto: You need my help. I will show you how to find food.

Narrator 1: Squanto taught the Pilgrims how to plant corn.

Squanto: Plant a fish head next to the seeds.
This will make the soil rich.
Your corn will grow well.

Narrator 2: Squanto taught the Pilgrims how to catch fish.

Squanto: I use a trap to catch fish.

Narrator 1: Squanto helped the Pilgrims find other foods, too.

Pilgrim 2: Thanks to Squanto, we have berries and turkey!

Narrator 2: Squanto got along well with the Pilgrims.
His people, the Wampanoag, did not.

Narrator 1: Squanto helped the Pilgrims talk
with the Wampanoag.
They made a peace treaty.

Chief: This peace treaty is a promise.
I promise that the Wampanoag
will not harm the Pilgrims.

Governor: We promise to protect the Wampanoag people.
We promise to treat them with kindness.

Narrator 2: In the fall, the Pilgrims' crops grew tall.
They found lots of fish and other foods.

Narrator 1: The Pilgrims held a big feast.
Chief Massasoit came with 90 Wampanoag.

Governor: We are thankful for such a fine harvest.
We are also thankful for Squanto.
He helped us in many ways.

The End

The Very First Leader

Characters

James Monroe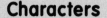

John Adams

Thomas Jefferson

Alexander Hamilton

George Washington

James Madison

**James
Monroe:** George Washington,
we have a new job for you.
We hope it is something
that you'll want to do.

**All but
George:** Will you be the first,
the very first leader?

Thomas: Please lead our country.
You will be the best.
Please say you'll do it.
Please say "Yes."

**All but
George:** You'll be the first,
the very first leader.

George: Gentlemen, listen.
I am getting old.
I do not think
I could be so bold.

John: You'll be a great leader.
That's easy to see.
You'll make our country
the best it can be!

**All but
George:** You'll be the first,
the very first leader.

Alexander: It will be great.
You'll be our king!
Then you will be able to do anything!

**All but
George:** You'll be the first,
the very first leader.

George: I don't want to be king.
That is not what we need.
Let the people be heard.
Let them help me to lead.

James Madison: What about president?
That sounds really good.
We'd help you make choices.
We promise we would.

George: All right, I will do it.
You have convinced me.
I will be the father
of our new country.

All: And you'll be the first,
the very first leader.
You'll be the first president
of our great land.

The End

Sewing Stars and Stripes

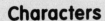

> **Characters**
>
> General George Washington   Robert Morris
> Betsy Ross   Seamstress 1
> Colonel George Ross   Seamstress 2

George Washington: Betsy, Betsy Ross!

Betsy: Yes?

George Ross: We have an important job for you.

Robert: We need a flag.

George Washington: We would like you to sew it.

Betsy: Why do you need a flag?

George Ross: The war is almost over.
Soon America will be free.

Robert: We will form our own country.
England will not own us anymore.

George Washington: Every country needs a flag.
Will you make one for us?

Betsy: Well, I'll try.

George Washington: Here is a picture of the flag we would like.

Betsy: The picture looks nice. I'll need some help.

Seamstress 1: I will help.

Seamstress 2: I will help, too.

Betsy: Come on, ladies.
We've got a flag to sew!

(The men leave. The women begin to sew.)

Seamstress 1: Why are we sewing 13 stars and 13 stripes?

Betsy: They stand for the 13 colonies
that will form our new country.

Seamstress 2: When people look at our flag,
they will think about America.

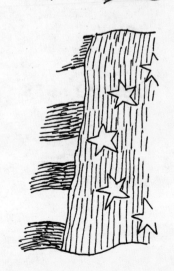

(Several weeks later)

Betsy: It's all finished!

George Washington: The flag is beautiful.
We will hang it for everyone to see.

All but Betsy: Hooray for Betsy Ross!

All: Hooray for stars and stripes!
Hooray for red, white, and blue!

The End

Planting Seeds of Kindness

Characters

Johnny Appleseed	Farmer's Wife
Farm Child 1	Farm Child 3
Farm Child 2	Farm Child 4
Farmer	Farm Child 5

Johnny: Apples are crunchy.
Apples are sweet.
Apples are very good to eat.

Farm Child 1: Hi there, stranger.
Who are you?

Johnny: I'm Johnny Appleseed.
How do you do?

Farm Child 2: What are you doing
here on our land?

Johnny: Planting apple seeds for you.
Come and give me a hand.

Farmer: Why do you do this?
Please give us a clue.

Farmer's Wife: Do you want money?
We have none to pay you.

Johnny: I like to help people.
That's all there is to it.
And people like apples.
That's why I do it.

Farm Child 3: Hey, Johnny Appleseed,
where are you going?

Johnny: To plant more seeds
so more trees can start growing.

Farm Child 4: Thank you, Johnny Appleseed!
Thanks for the seeds!

Farm Child 5: Thanks for being nice.
That is what the world needs.

Johnny: Take care of your trees,
and they will grow tall.
And be nice to people.
That's the best gift of all!

The End

Good Old Abe, Honest Abe

> **Characters**
>
> Abe (Abraham Lincoln)
> Narrators 1 to 5

Abe: I was born in a cabin made of logs.

All: Good old Abe, honest Abe.

Abe: I lived in the woods with raccoons and frogs.

All: Good old Abe, honest Abe.

Narrator 1: He liked to help people in need.

All: Good old Abe, honest Abe.

Narrator 2: His favorite thing to do was read.

All: Good old Abe, honest Abe.

Narrator 3: He told stories and funny jokes.

All: Good old Abe, honest Abe.

Narrator 4: He was liked by lots of folks.

All: Good old Abe, honest Abe.

Abe: I saw some slaves in New Orleans.

All: Good old Abe, honest Abe.

Abe: It was the saddest sight I'd ever seen.

All: Good old Abe, honest Abe.

Narrator 5: To the White House he was sent . . .

All: Good old Abe, honest Abe.

Narrator 1: . . . to be our sixteenth president.

All: Good old Abe, honest Abe.

Narrator 2: He found a way to set slaves free.

All: Good old Abe, honest Abe.

Narrator 3: He changed the laws for liberty.

All: Good old Abe, honest Abe.

Narrator 4: Now owning slaves was not allowed.

All: Good old Abe, honest Abe.

Narrator 5: Thank you, Abe. You've made us proud!

All: Good old Abe, honest Abe!

The End

Follow the North Star

Harriet: All aboard for the Underground Railroad!
Please come and follow me.
I will lead you North
to a place where you'll be free.

Slave 1: Is there really a train
that can help set us free?

Slave 2: Is it really underground?
Where could it be?

Harriet: It's not underground
and it's not a real train.
It's a path we will walk on
through wind, hail, and rain.

Slave 3: Look up in the sky!
Do you see the North Star?
We must follow its light.
It will take us quite far.

Slave 4: We don't want to be seen.
We'll walk only at night.
We'll hide and sleep
when the sky becomes light.

Harriet: Today we will stay in a house on a farm.
My friends will hide us
and keep us from harm.

(Several days later)

Harriet: Please remember that freedom is near.
We all must stay quiet
so no one will hear.

Slave 5: We've made it!
We stand on free soil at last.

Slave 6: We are no longer slaves.
That's a thing of the past.

Harriet: Last stop is freedom!
Now you will see.
Being free is the best way to be!

The End

Have You Heard the News?

Narrator 1: Have you heard the news
across the land?

Narrator 2: Women can vote!

Narrator 3: Isn't it grand?

Narrator 4: How did this happen?

Narrator 5: How could this be?

Narrator 1: It's because of Susan B. Anthony!

Narrator 2: Susan B. Anthony worked for so long.

Narrator 3: She helped to change laws
that she thought were wrong.

Susan: I know that women are equal to men.

Narrator 4: Yet women weren't treated
as equals back then.

Susan: If women could vote,
our ideas would be heard.
I'm going to change things.
I give you my word!

Narrator 5: Susan called to women across the U.S.

Susan: Do you want equal rights?

Narrator 1: And the women said "Yes!"

All: Now women can vote.
Their ideas can be heard.
Susan B. Anthony helped change things.
She kept her word.

Now this country is better
than it used to be
because of Susan B. Anthony.

The End

Carver Saves the Day!

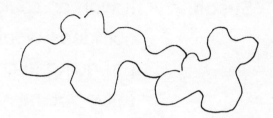

Farmer 1: There are problems on our farms.
We cannot grow our crops.

Farmer 2: Let's ask George Washington Carver for help.
We hear that he is tops!

Farmer 3: Mr. Carver, our cotton will not grow.

Farmer 4: Bugs are eating all our plants.
Please tell us what you know.

George: Peanuts are the answer,
and sweet potatoes, too.
Each of these improves the soil.
They will work for you.

Farmer 5: Plant peanuts and sweet potatoes?
How good will they be?

Farmer 1: Not everybody likes
to eat those foods, you see.

George: Peanuts can be used
to make paper and ink,
shaving cream, shampoo,
and even milk that you can drink!

Farmer 2: What about sweet potatoes?
What can they do?

George: You can use them to make vinegar, syrup, and glue!

(Many months later)

Farmer 3: We're glad we planted the new crops.
They are helpful to our land.

Farmer 4: Thanks for taking the time
to help us understand.

Farmer 5: Peanuts and sweet potatoes
have kept our land from harm.
You have saved so many families.
And you have saved our farms.

All Farmers: George Washington Carver had the answer.
He helped show us the way.
He told us what to plant,
and he helped to save the day!

The End

Like a Bird in the Sky

Characters

Birds 1 to 8
Orville Wright
Wilbur Wright

Bird 1: Have you heard about Orville and Wilbur Wright?

Bird 2: These brothers want to fly like a kite.

Bird 3: Everyone knows that people can't fly!

Bird 4: But they want to fly like a bird in the sky!

All Birds: Like a bird, like a bird,
like a bird in the sky!

Orville: Now we are ready to try our flight.

Wilbur: We hope that it will go just right.

38

Orville and Wilbur: We think we can do it! We're going to try.
We hope we can fly like a bird in the sky.

All Birds: Like a bird, like a bird,
like a bird in the sky!

Bird 5: Look at those two.
The brothers were right.

Bird 6: They can fly through the air
just like a kite.

Bird 7: Their plane has a motor.
It even has wings.

Bird 8: It can carry a person.
Just look at that thing!

Orville: We did it! We did it!
We really can fly!

Wilbur: We really can fly like a bird in the sky!

All: Like a bird, like a bird,
like a bird in the sky!

The End

Helen's Favorite Word

Characters

Helen Keller	Narrator 2
Mom (Helen's mother)	Dad (Helen's father)
Narrator 1	Anne Sullivan

Helen: My world is silent.
My world is dark.

Mom: Helen can't see the flowers
or hear a dog bark.

Narrator 1: Helen's parents tried to help,
but they didn't know what to do.

Narrator 2: Then they had an idea to try something new.

Dad: Helen, we have a surprise for you.

15 Plays About Famous Americans for Emergent Readers   Scholastic Professional Books

Anne: My name is Anne Sullivan.
                I'm here to help you.

Mom: We are glad you are here.
                How will you help Helen understand?

Anne: I'll teach her to spell words
                in the palm of her hand.

Helen: What is she doing?
                She's touching my hand.
                She's tracing some shapes
                that I don't understand.

Anne: D-O-L-L.
                C-U-P.

Narrator 1: Anne had lots of patience.
                 She worked very hard.

Narrator 2: One day she brought Helen
                 out into the yard.

Anne: Let's try it again.
You're close. I can tell.
Now feel what is coming
out of this well.

W-A-T-E-R.

Helen: W-A-T-E-R.
Water! It's water!
I get it! I do!
The letters spell water!
I understand you!

Anne: Helen cannot hear
and she cannot see.
But now she can spell words
and that will set her free.

Dad: Thank you, Anne, for all that you've done.
Now that Helen knows words,
her new life has begun.

Helen: My very favorite word, by far,
is T-E-A-C-H-E-R!

The End

15 Plays About Famous Americans for Emergent Readers Scholastic Professional Books

He Had a Dream

Characters

Teacher
Students 1–5

Teacher: Martin Luther King, Jr., had an important dream.
It was not a dream you have when you're sleeping.
It was a different kind of dream.

Student 1: His dream was his goal for all people.

Student 2: His dream was his greatest hope and wish.

All: He had a dream.

Student 3: In his dream, all people were treated as equals.

Student 4: In his dream, all people were free.

All: He had a dream.

Student 5: In his dream, people treated one another
with respect.

Student 1: In his dream, people did not judge one another by the color of their skin.

All: He had a dream.

Student 2: In his dream, people worked together.

Student 3: In his dream, people lived together in peace.

All: He had a dream.

Teacher: Martin Luther King, Jr., wanted others to know about his dream.

Student 4: He spoke about his dream. He wrote about his dream.

Student 5: He told people how they could make our country a better place.

All: Martin Luther King, Jr., knew that when all people shared his dream, his dream would come true.

The End

Rosa Parks Rides the Bus

> **Characters**
>
> Passengers 1 to 5
> Bus Driver
> Rosa Parks

Passenger 1:   Rosa Parks got on the bus.

All: And the bus rolled on and on.

Passenger 2:   She took a seat right in the middle.

All: And the bus rolled on and on.

Passenger 3:   Then some white people got on the bus.

All: And the bus rolled on and on.

Passenger 4:   They did not have a place to sit.

All: And the bus rolled on and on.

Passenger 5:   The bus driver spoke to Rosa.

All: And the bus rolled on and on.

Bus Driver: You must go stand in the back.

All: And the bus rolled on and on.

Passenger 1:   Rosa said:

Rosa: I will not go!

All: And the bus stopped!

Passenger 2:   Rosa would not move.
She was put in jail.

Passenger 3:   African-American people heard what happened.
They stopped riding the bus.

Passenger 4:   This showed that they
did not agree with the rules.

Passenger 5:   Finally the law was changed. From then on,
Rosa did not need to give up her seat.

All: Now the bus rolls on and on.

The End

15 Plays About Famous Americans for Emergent Readers   Scholastic Professional Books

A View From Space

Characters

Ground Crew Workers 1 to 6
Sally Ride

Worker 1: Earth to Sally Ride!
Come in, Sally Ride!

Worker 2: Sally Ride, you are the first
American woman in space.
What is it like to be in such a place?

Sally: This is Sally.
I read you loud and clear.
The world looks beautiful
from way up here.

Worker 3: Tell us, Sally.
What do you see?

Sally: I see bright orange deserts
and sparkling seas.

Worker 4: How does it feel to be
so far from the ground?

Sally: I feel as light as a feather.
I'm floating around!

Worker 5: When you're up there in space,
what do you do?

Sally: I run tests and I do research, too.

Worker 6: What would you tell children
who want to fly?

Sally: You can be an astronaut.
Give it a try!

The End

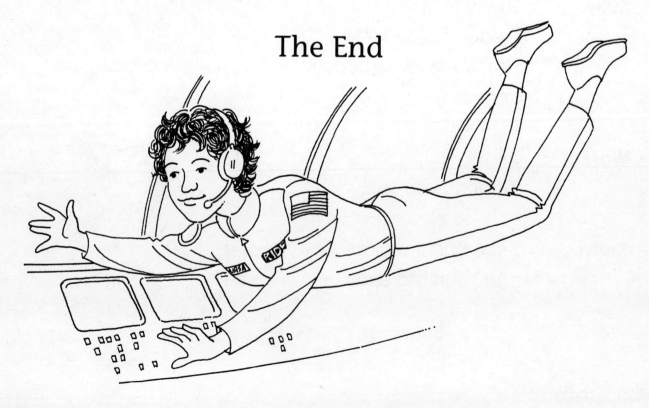